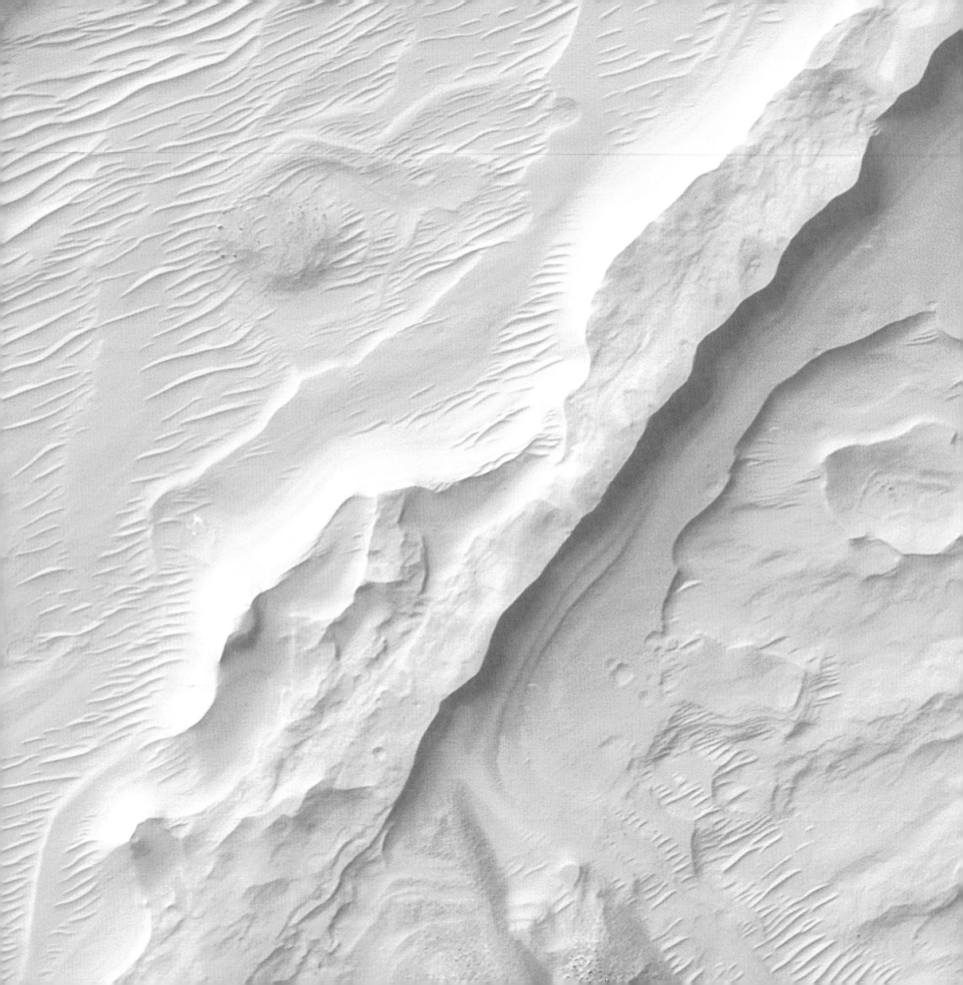

MARS IS

To Mike, the center of my universe
—S. S.

The author wishes to thank the following HiRISE experts from the University of Arizona's Lunar and Planetary Lab for their assistance with this project: Ari Espinoza, HiRISE Outreach Coordinator; Dr. Matthew Chojnacki, Associate Staff Scientist; and Dr. Shane Byrne, Professor, Assistant Department Head.

Published by
PEACHTREE PUBLISHING COMPANY INC.
1700 Chattahoochee Avenue
Atlanta, Georgia 30318-2112
www.peachtree-online.com

Text © 2021 by Suzanne Slade
Photo credits
NASA/Jet Propulsion Laboratory/Malin Space Science Systems: 4–5
NASA/Jet Propulsion Laboratory-California Institute of Technology/
University of Arizona: 6–7, 11, 16–17, 18–19, 20–21, 22, 25, 29, 33, 34, 37, 38
NASA/Jet Propulsion Laboratory/University of Arizona: 8, 12, 15, 26, 30
NASA/Jet Propulsion Laboratory/Kennedy Space Center/Lockheed Martin
Space System: 43
NASA/Jet Propulsion Laboratory/Ball Aerospace: 44
NASA/Jet Propulsion Laboratory-California Institute of Technology: 47

Edited by Kathy Landwehr
Design and composition by Nicola Simmonds Carmack and Adela Pons

Printed in January 2021 by Toppan Leefung in China
10 9 8 7 6 5 4 3 2 1
First Edition
ISBN 978-1-68263-188-1

Cataloging-in-Publication Data is available from the Library of Congress.

MARS IS

Stark Slopes, Silvery Snow, and Startling Surprises

SUZANNE SLADE

PEACHTREE

ATLANTA

People have wondered about the
mysterious planet of Mars for centuries.

Over time, scientists discovered Mars
has weather and seasons, just like Earth.
But curious earthlings wanted to know more.

So scientists built a powerful camera and
launched it on a long journey, millions of miles
through space, to take a closer look at Mars.

Several months later, the camera sent
fascinating photos back to Earth
that show us what Mars is.

Mars is buried bedrock,

Buried bedrock, which is often hidden beneath the loose, fine-grained material covering the surface of Mars, creates a solid foundation for this magnificent planet. Here's a rare glimpse of exposed bedrock with its gorgeous rocky layers.

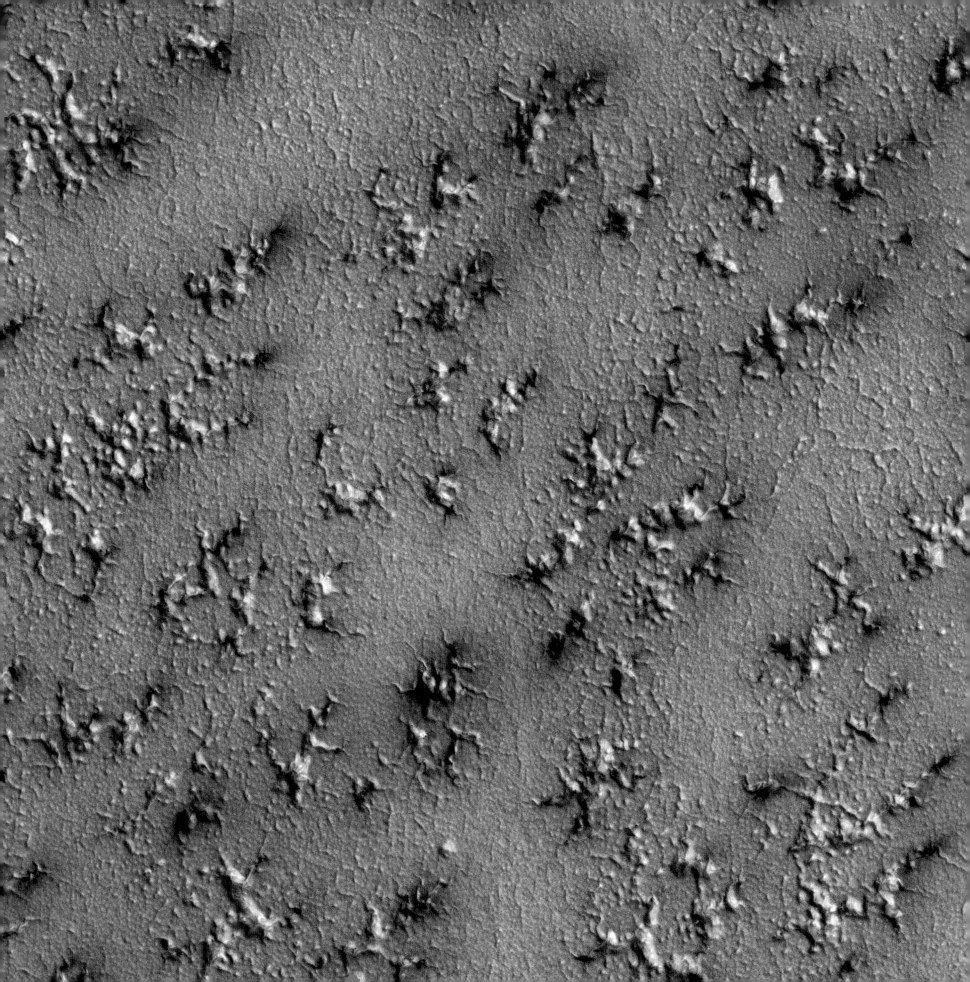

Like Earth, Mars has two polar ice caps. Unlike those on Earth, the Martian caps contain dry ice (frozen carbon dioxide) rather than water. In spring, more sunlight starts to shine on the South Pole and warms its surface. Soon, bubbling gas rises from the ground and carves channels in the ice.

bubbling gas,

and mighty mesas.

Surrounded by blowing sand dunes, this quarter-mile-wide mesa has a flat top and steep sides. It is on the west end of the solar system's largest canyon, Valles Marineris, which is more than four times the size of the Grand Canyon!

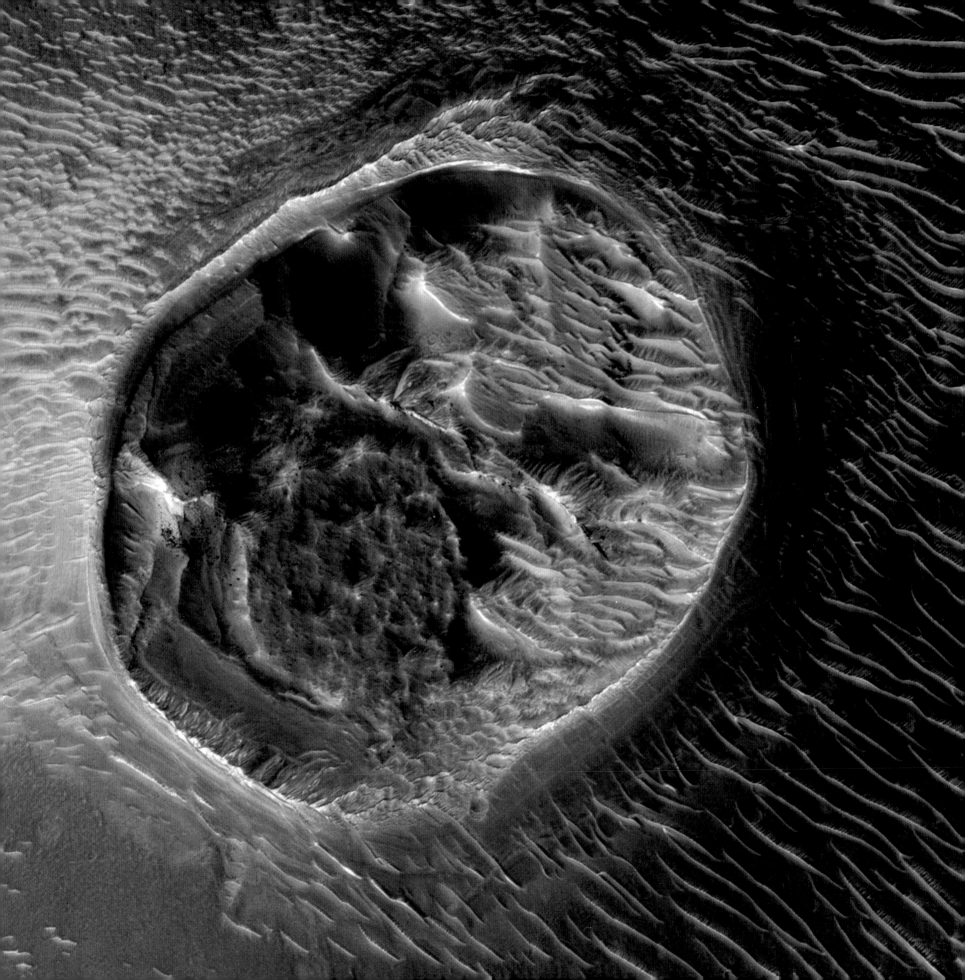

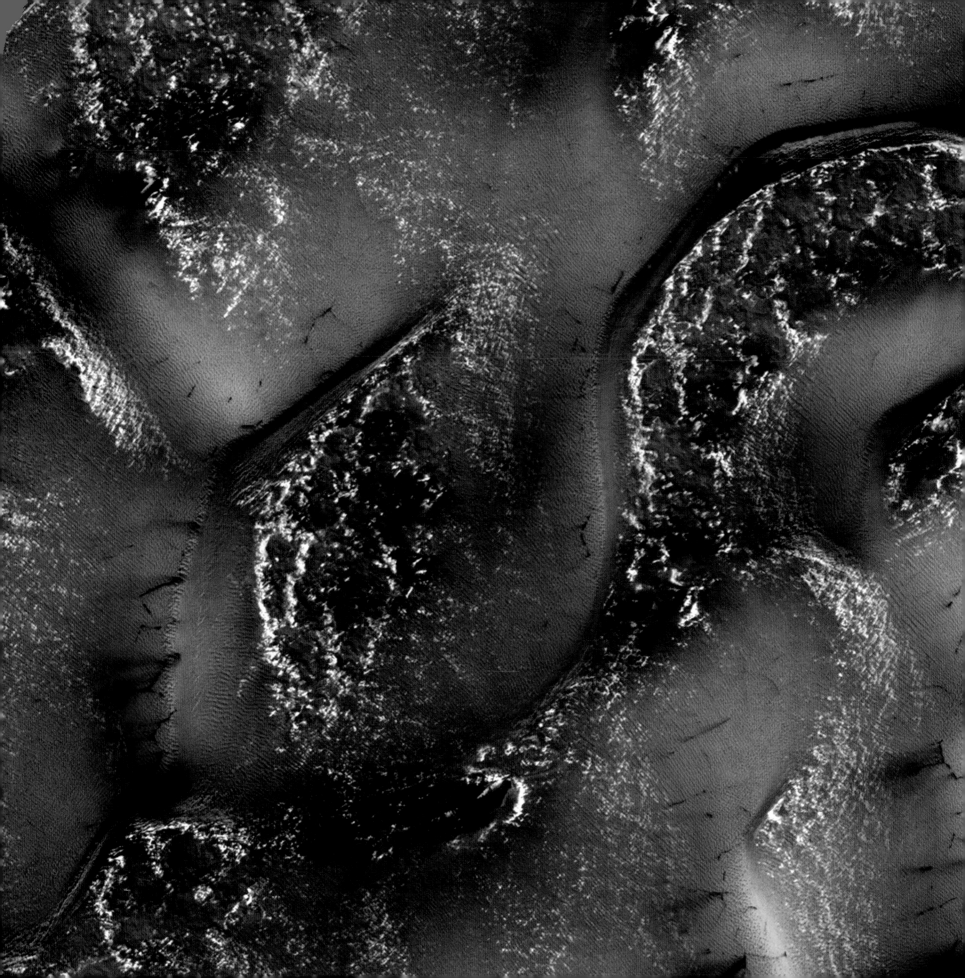

During winter, these sandy dunes in the Northern Hemisphere of Mars become covered with snow and big sheets of dry ice. When the sun shines in springtime, the ice begins to crack. Soon, gas escapes up through the cracks and carries dark sand to the surface, painting beautiful, swirling designs.

Mars is slippery snow and ice,

sandy, windswept dunes,

The dunes of Mars are on the move! Winds blew this sandy dune, located inside Lyot Crater, into mesmerizing ripples and waves. Scientists calculate some dunes travel over three feet (about one meter) in a Martian year, which is 687 Earth days.

and craters carved by meteorite crashes.

This colossal crater was created when a meteorite collided with Mars. The material around the edge is called ejecta because it was ejected by the explosive force of the crash. Scientists believe it is a relatively new crater due to its crisp, sharp rim.

Mars is
steep cliffs

The rim of Krupac Crater is surrounded by steep cliffs, while large gullies run down its inner slope. Although Krupac is considered a relatively young impact crater, it has exposed ancient Mars bedrock.

and canyons,

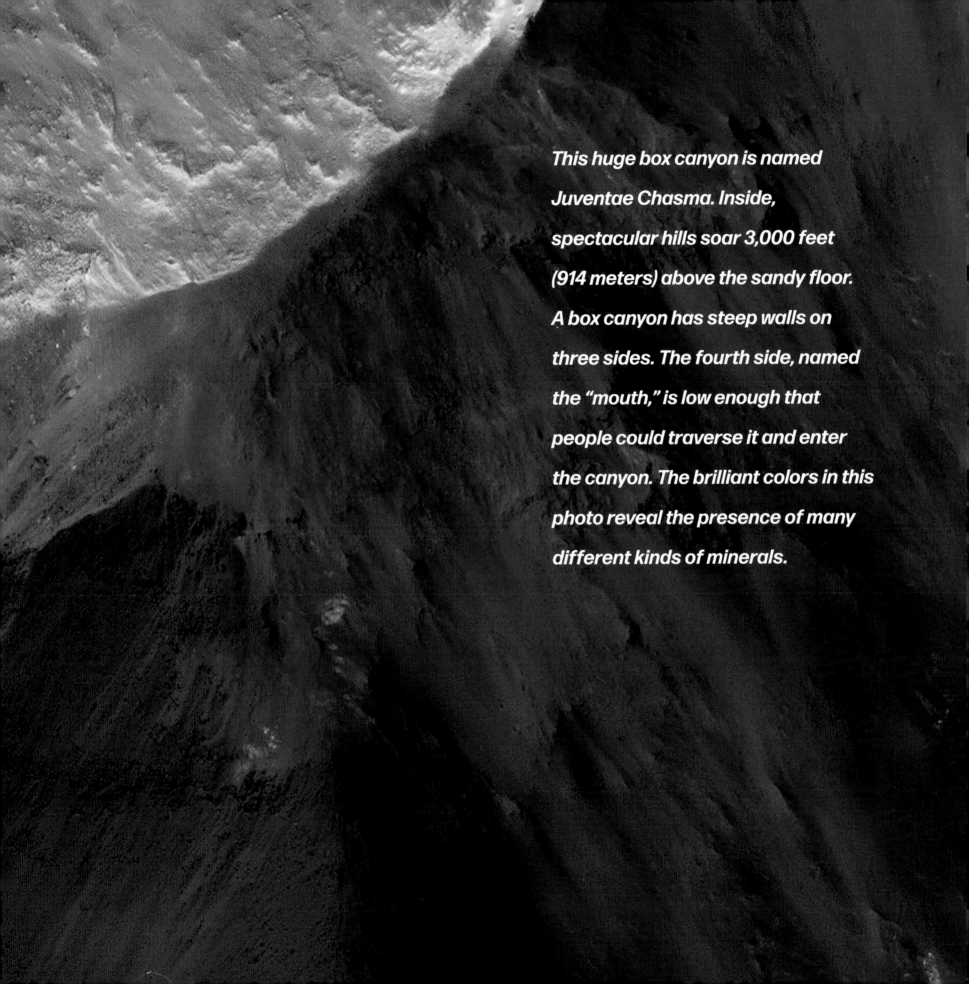

This huge box canyon is named Juventae Chasma. Inside, spectacular hills soar 3,000 feet (914 meters) above the sandy floor. A box canyon has steep walls on three sides. The fourth side, named the "mouth," is low enough that people could traverse it and enter the canyon. The brilliant colors in this photo reveal the presence of many different kinds of minerals.

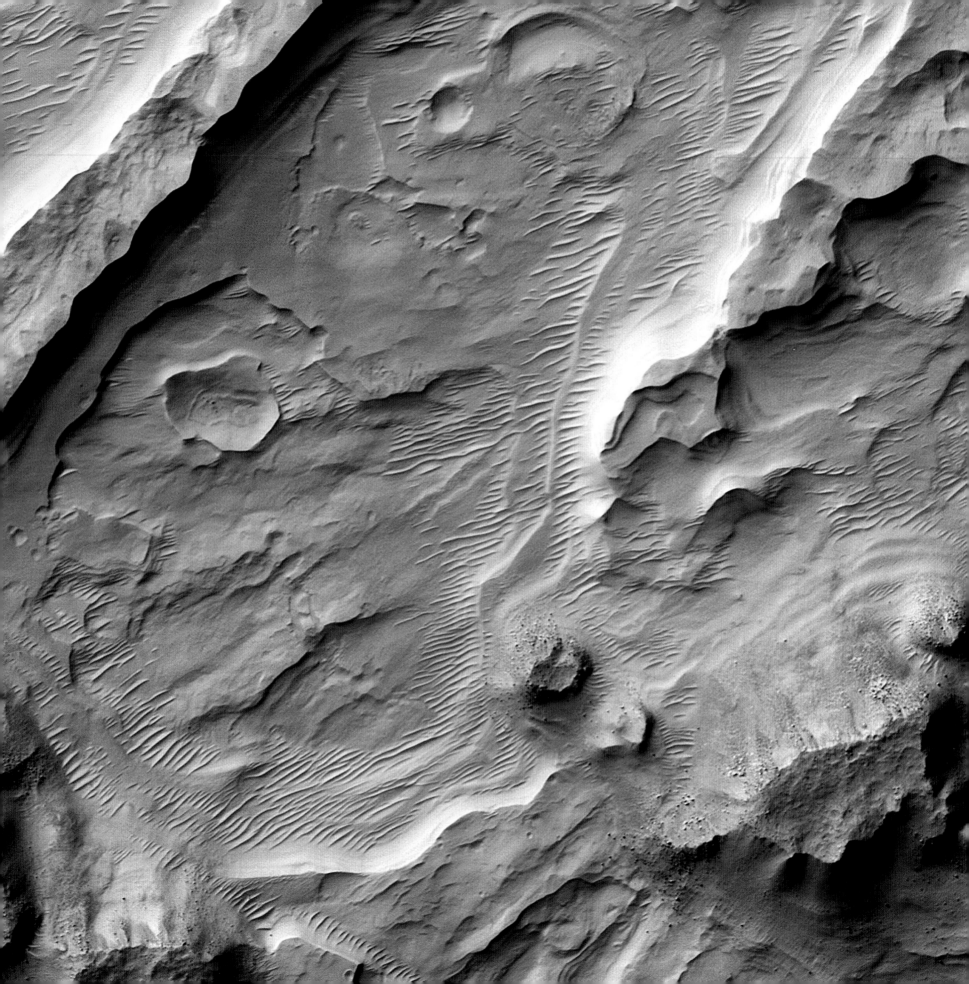

wide fans

Scientists believe that these fan-shaped deposits, called alluvial fans, are proof that water flowed on Mars long ago. "Alluvial" refers to clay, silt, sand, and gravel left behind by moving water. The tall ridges protruding above the fans are thought to be ancient channels that once carried streams of water.

and ridges,

This dry valley is filled with lovely linear ridges created by wind. These tall ridges have small, sandy ripples extending downward, which gives them a feathery appearance.

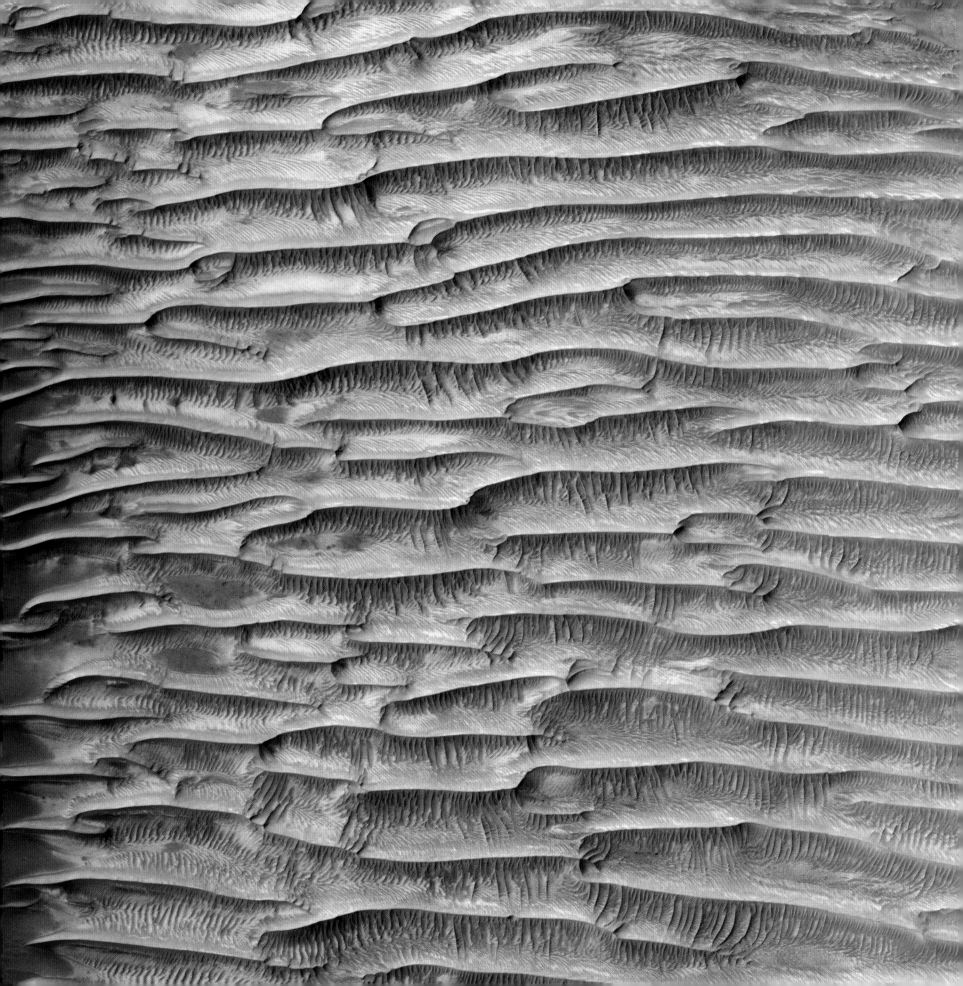

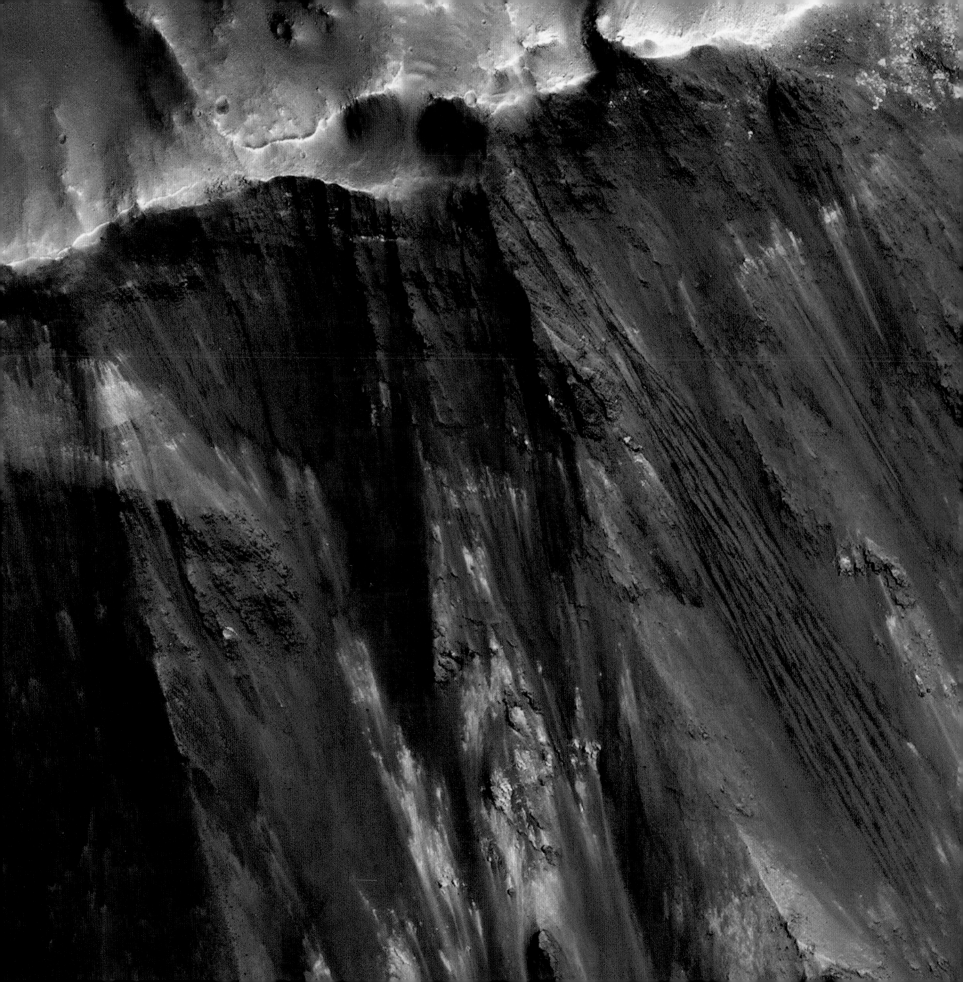

An incoming asteroid, meteorite, or comet created this impact crater. Its steep, stark slopes lead to sudden avalanches of debris and rockfalls. After each avalanche, a fresh, dust-free surface is exposed, revealing different types of rock.

stark slopes

and landslides.

The tallest volcano in the solar system, Olympus Mons, is located on Mars. No longer active, it stands about 15.5 miles (25 kilometers) high. Enormous landslides falling down the giant volcano created this rocky block. Over time, wind eroded it into a scenic layered landscape.

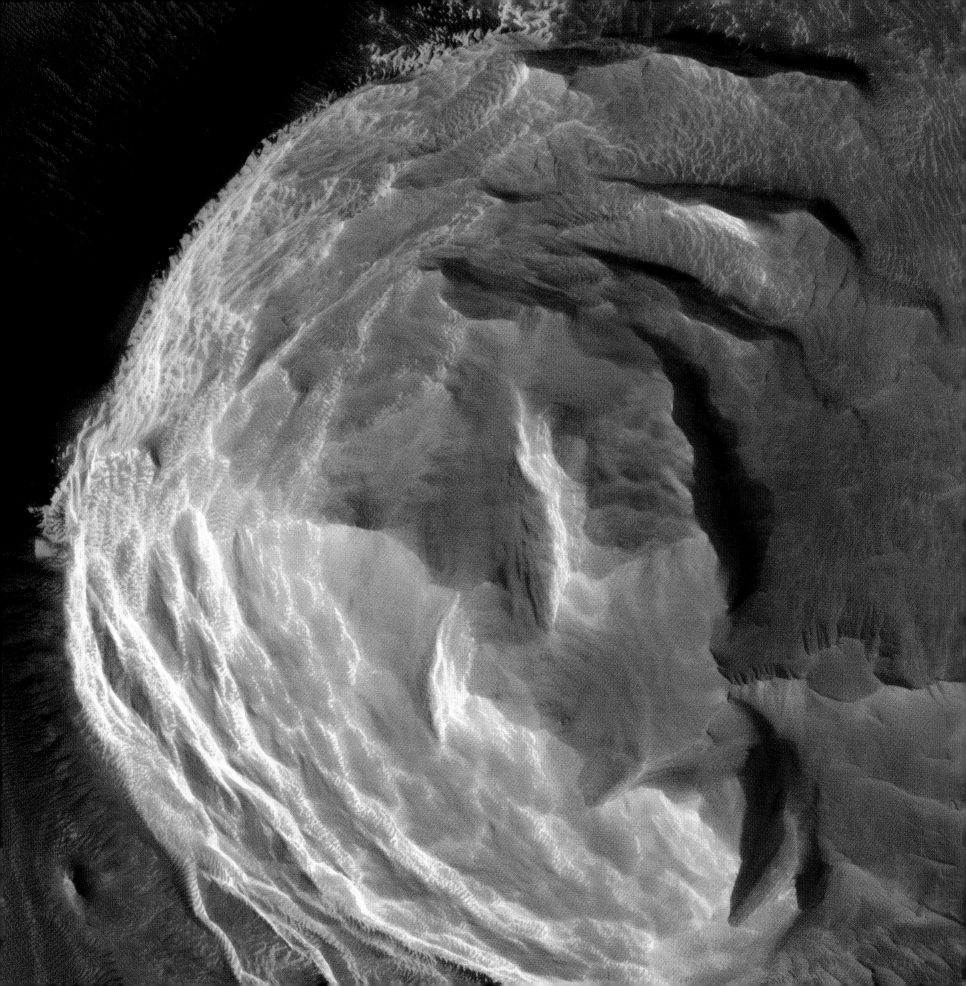

Mars is shifting

A process called sublimation, where solid ice turns into a gas, occurs on Mars every spring. As sunshine begins to turn the ice on these northern sandy dunes to gas, dark sand or dirt peeks out through small cracks in the remaining ice. The pink color indicates where Martian dust has settled on the ice.

An explosion of dusty material caused by the impact of an incoming object created this fresh crater. The crater measures about 100 feet (30 meters) in diameter, a little more than the distance between two bases on a baseball field. The large, rayed blast zone around it extends over 9 miles (14.5 kilometers) from its center.

and changing,

heaving,

Sand isn't the only thing moving on Mars. Large boulders are moving too! This is caused by frost heave, a movement that occurs when the planet's surface freezes and thaws as it orbits the sun. Frost heave brings rocks to the surface and organizes them into neatly spaced piles.

rearranging,

Wind is always rearranging the surface of Mars. When wind blows sand in one direction for a period of time, sand particles carve long, thin rocky ridges called yardangs. Flanked by sand-filled channels on each side, a yardang usually points in the direction the wind was blowing when it was created.

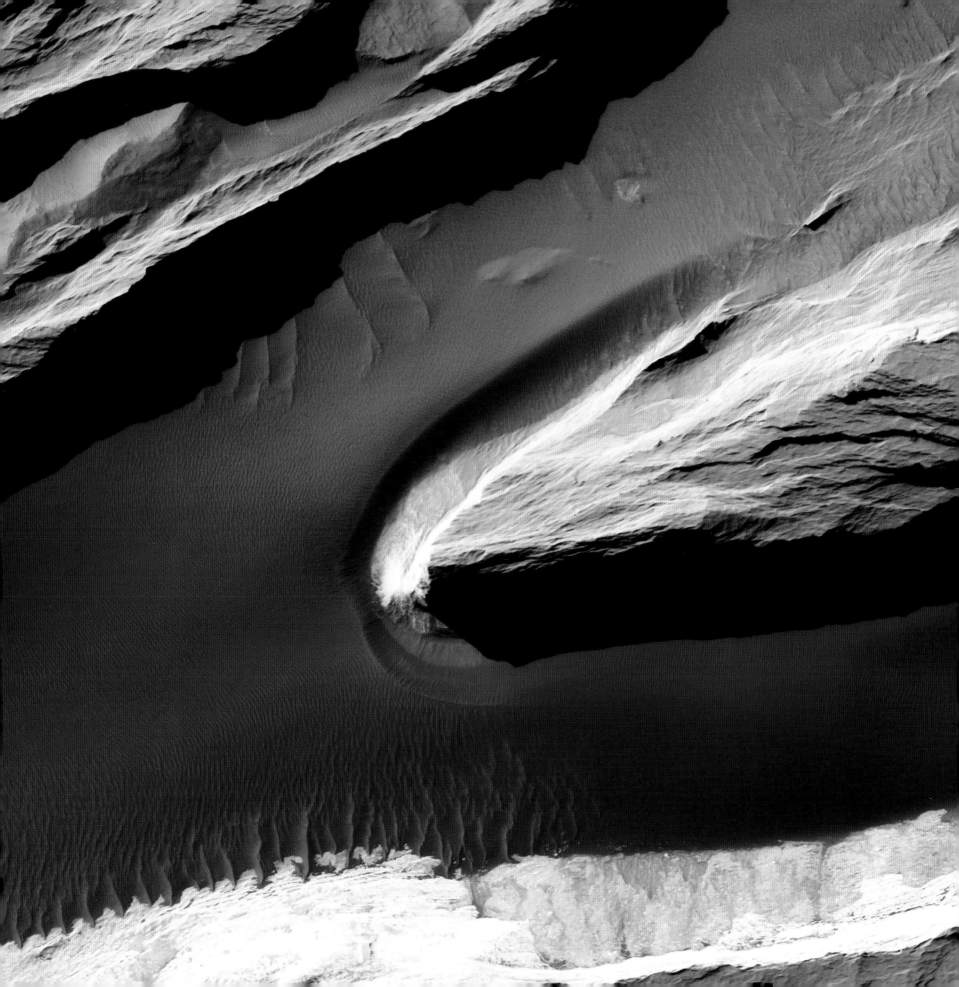

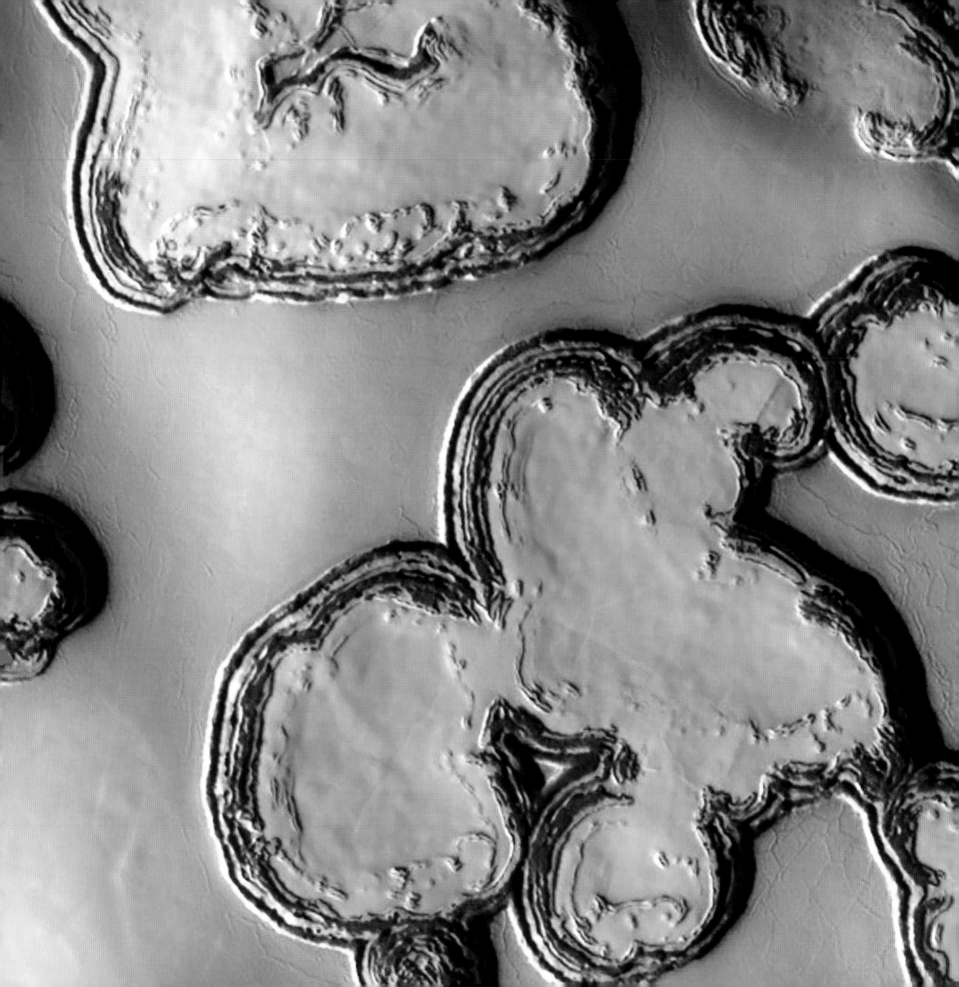

completely breathtaking!

During a cold winter on Mars, carbon dioxide in the atmosphere freezes and turns into solid ice. Near the frigid South Pole, some of this ice accumulates into large, roundish-shaped slabs about 10 feet (3 meters) thick. Scientists believe the walls surrounding the ice pits in this photo are colored by dust trapped inside the ice.

Mars is more amazing than anyone ever imagined!

Mars is an active, busy place where things are always changing. Dust storms, incoming meteorites, rising and falling temperatures, trembling Marsquakes, and other factors are constantly transforming the landscape of this stunning planet!

Launching the Mission to Mars

NASA's mighty Atlas V rocket blasted off from Cape Canaveral, Florida, on August 12, 2005, carrying important cargo—the Mars Reconnaissance Orbiter (MRO) spacecraft with its HiRISE camera.

The mission launch date was carefully considered because the distance between Earth and Mars changes as both planets orbit the Sun. During "Close Approach," Mars and Earth are the closest they will get to each another—about 33.9 million miles (54.5 million kilometers) apart. The farthest the two planets move away from each other is 249 million miles (400.73 kilometers).

After many calculations, NASA determined a launch period for the mission—between August 10 and 30, 2005. During that time period, scientists continually evaluated the weather, equipment, and other factors. On August 12, all systems were "go" and the Atlas rocket lifted off. That day, Mars was relatively close to Earth—about 71 million miles (114.3 kilometers) away.

Seven months after leaving Earth, the MRO spacecraft finally reached its destination and began orbiting Mars in March 2006. The HiRISE camera sent its first test photos back to Earth a few weeks later, and has continued taking incredible pictures of Mars ever since!

HiRISE: The Spectacular Space Camera

The remarkable photos in this book were taken by HiRISE (High Resolution Imaging Science Experiment)—the most advanced camera ever sent to another planet. It is riding on a spacecraft named MRO, which began orbiting Mars in March 2006.

Soaring about 200 miles (322 kilometers) above the surface of Mars, HiRISE uses a telescopic lens to take highly detailed pictures. On average, it transmits the photos 140 million miles (225 million kilometers) through space (which takes 15 minutes) to eager scientists on Earth. HiRISE has taken more than 60,000 photos. This powerful camera is still circling Mars and sending new photos home.

Unlike ordinary cameras on Earth, HiRISE creates enhanced color photos, which include color information people can't see. Eyes perceive color due to wavelength of light. Human eyes see light wavelengths from about 390-700 nanometers (1 nanometer = 1 billionth of a meter). HiRISE photographs wavelengths from 400-1,000 nm. Since our eyes can't detect color above 700 nm, those longer wavelengths are represented in the photographs with colors people can see. Also, in some enhanced photos the visible colors are made brighter or more intense. HiRISE pictures allow viewers to see different rocks, soil, and textures on Mars to learn more about this fascinating planet.

More about Mars

Like Earth, Mars is a dynamic planet that has wind, clouds, and weather that change with the seasons. The temperature on Mars ranges from a frigid -190 Fahrenheit (-123 Celsius) at night to 86F (30C) during the day. Its average temperature is well below freezing, -80F (-62 C).

Mars is the fourth planet from the sun, while Earth is third. Instead of one moon, Mars has two—Phobos and Deimos. Mars is bigger than our moon, but is only one-sixth the size of Earth. Often called the Red Planet, Mars gets its reddish color from bits of iron in the soil.

HiRISE photos reveal many different land formations on Mars, such as sand dunes, canyons, craters, volcanoes, and lava flows. Those detailed pictures are also helping scientists study potential landing sites for future visits to Earth's next-door-neighbor, Mars.

Highlights of the Exploration of Mars

1600s Mars is first discovered by early astronomers using telescopes.

May 30, 1971 USA launches Mariner 9, the first spacecraft to orbit Mars, which maps 85 percent of its surface.

December 2, 1971 The USSR's Mars 3 lander makes the first successful landing on the planet's surface.

July 20, 1976 Viking 1 becomes the first US mission to land on Mars. It sends back photos of the surface.

November 7, 1996 USA launches Mars Global Surveyor. It later orbits Mars and takes photos to study topography, gravity, and weather.

December 25, 2003 Mars Express, a mission launched by the European Space Agency, begins orbiting Mars. Its main goal: search for water below the surface while circling the planet.

January 2004 US rovers Spirit and Opportunity land on Mars. The rovers traverse the surface and send home data about climate, geography, photos, and video.

August 12, 2005 USA launches an Atlas V rocket, carrying the MRO and HiRISE camera.

March 10, 2006 MRO begins orbiting Mars.

March 24, 2006 HiRISE transmits its first photo, the southern highlands of Mars, which helps scientists test camera settings.

March 10–November 2006 MRO gradually brakes to slow down and move into orbit closer to the surface of Mars.

November 2006–present HiRISE sends thousands of detailed Mars photos to Earth.

September 24, 2014 India's Mars Orbiter Mission (MOM) begins orbiting Mars, becoming the first nation to enter the planet's orbit on its first attempt.

July 20, 2020 Japan launches the United Arab Emirates satellite called Hope, which plans to orbit Mars and study its climate and atmosphere.

July 23, 2020 China launches Tianwen-1, a Mars mission which includes both an orbiter and a rover.

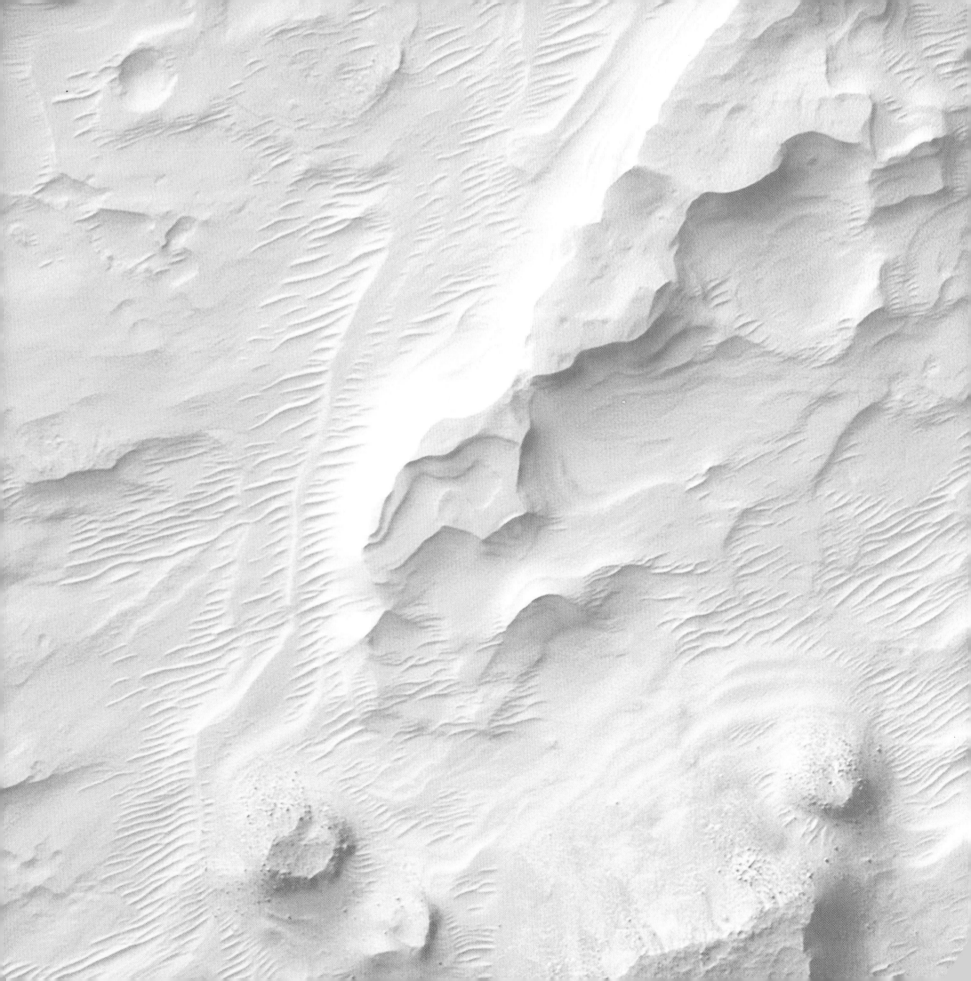

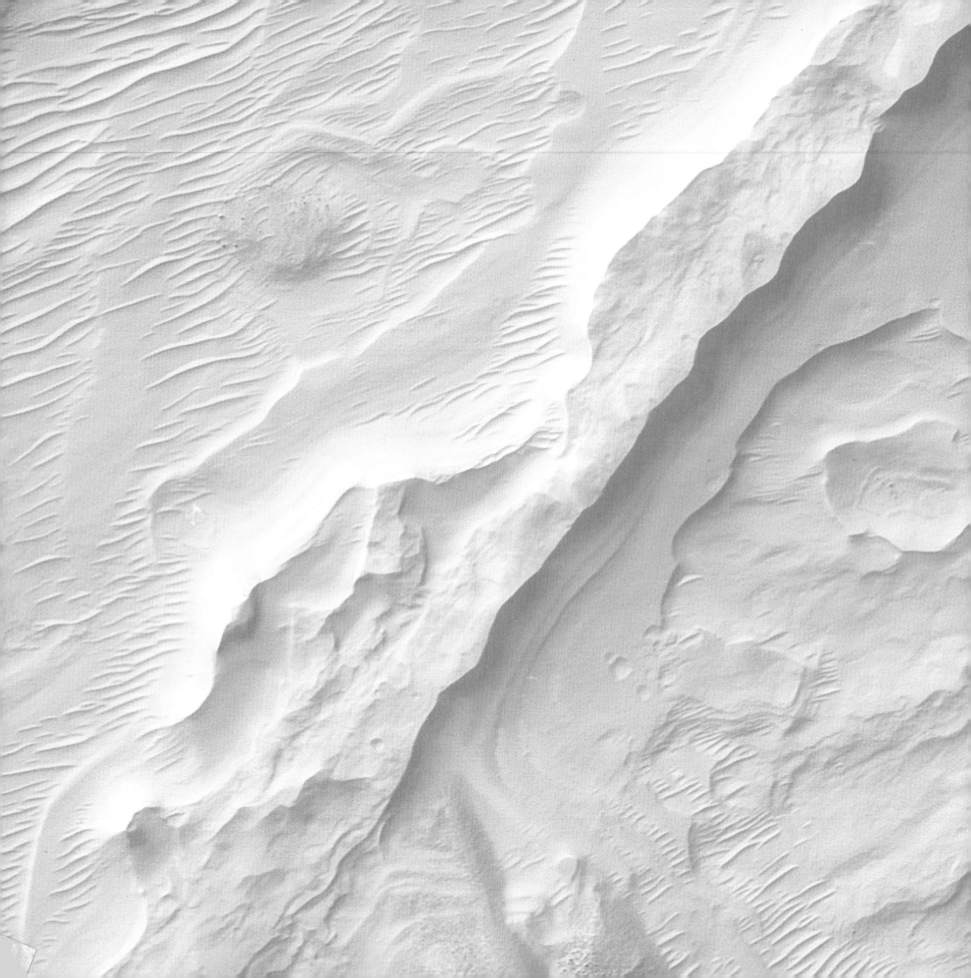